Let it grow

by Susie Poole

Peach's glasses belonged to **Scarlet**'s Grandpa. No-one knew the **big**, brown book like **Grandpa**. When **Grandpa** read it, the words **leapt** off the page and **shone** like stars in the night sky.

Peach is of course a **very** special cat and the glasses now belong to him. With the glasses on his **nose**, **Peach** can dive **deep** into the **big**, brown book and bring it to life, just like **Grandpa**.

Let it grow

THIS BOOK BELONGS TO:

Scarlet was having a lovely time, sticking and gluing. There were all kinds of pictures to choose from.

Mummy had cut them out and spread them over the kitchen table.

Scarlet liked the sunflowers best.

one UP here,

one DOWN there

and one on Peach's nose!

Scarlet had all kinds of 'here and there' ideas about where to stick sunfLOWers!

Mummy decided it was time to go shopping.

Scarlet didn't want to go shopping. She took ages to put on her shoes.

PEACH was excited.

He skipped and
purrrrrred out of the
door and all the way
to the pet shop,
where Mummy
wanted to buy
some seeds.

'I need seeds for the **birds** that visit our garden,' said mummy to the pet shop man.

'Sunflower seeds' would be best,' he replied.

'**Full** of goodness!'

The seeds were black and white and small.

'You could POP some of these into the ground and get SUNflowers too,' he added.

The seeds felt lovely in **ScarLEt**'s hand.
She wanted mummy to help plant them,
but mummy said,

'Not NOW, **ScarLet**,
I'm busY'.

ScarLEt felt the tickle
of **PeacH**'s little
wet nose on her leg.

He led her to the
patch of bare
brown soil
near the
greenhouse.

SCARLET took charge!
'Make a hole,
    POP in the seeds,
        COVER them up.'

PEACH covered them up.
SCARLET gave them
    a GOOD drink,
        and
    then
waited.

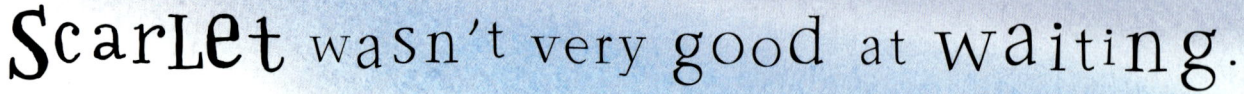

Scarlet wasn't very good at waiting.
She stood on ONE leg...
and then the OTHER...

Still nothing happened.

Thinking she would check if the little seeds were OK, she picked up her trowel and knelt down to dig.

But there **sat Peach**, right on top of the spot where the seeds had been planted!

'Move!' said Scarlet.

'NO!' purred Peach.

'I mean it!' said Scarlet.

'Me too!' scowled Peach.

Scarlet was cross. She wanted to SHOUT!

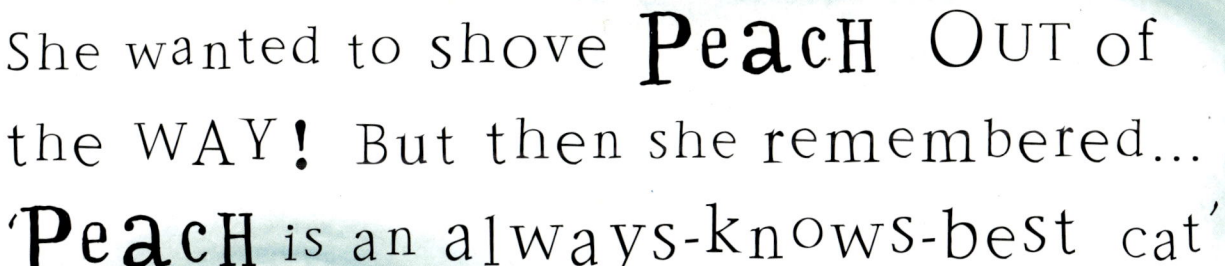

She wanted to shove **PEACH** OUT of the WAY! But then she remembered... 'PEACH is an always-knows-best cat'.

So when a beautiful butterfly flit-fluttered past, **ScarLet** chased it around the garden.

Days and weeks slowly passed.

On sunny days
Scarlet thought,
'this is good
for my seeds'.

On rainy days
Scarlet thought,
'this is probably good
for my seeds too'.

On windy days
she wanted to bring them inside.

It was then that
she would look at
PEACH smiling –
quietly watching through
the window.

She knew everything was
going to be okay.

One day, whilst playing
in the garden,
a beautiful butterfly
flit-fluttered past.

Scarlet skipped after it and stopped suddenly
by the patch of bare, brown soil near the
greenhouse. There she saw four, fresh green
shoots pushing up out of the ground.

Soon they were
as tall
as Peach.

Then they were as tall as Scarlet.

But later...

They stretched right over the top of mummy's head!

Everyone loved **ScarLet's** sunflowers!

They made **people** smile as they walked by.

The boy from next door gasped
as he stood beneath them and
marvelled when SCarLet said
they came from...
...a tiny seed!

As the weather began to get colder, the sunflowers changed from bright, sunny yellow to a dingy, dull brown.

Scarlet was a little bit sad until she remembered the seeds.

Each **sunflower** was full of them.
Black and white and small.

She would give some to
the boy next door,
keep some in a **jar**,

and use the rest
to **feed** the **birds**
right through the
winter.

That night, **Scarlet** put the
jar of seeds by her bed.

She lifted the **big** brown, book
down from the shelf, where it sat,
waiting to be opened.

She put the **special** glasses on the end
of **Peach's** nose.

'Peach, PEACH!
Take a look,
In the wonderful, helpful,
big, brown book.
Open the pages.
What do you
see?
Tell me lots more,
about how God
loves me.'

PEACH dived onto the pages.
They turned and flicked
until stopping at the
right place.

'Trust in God with all your heart,' said the big, brown book, 'and don't depend on what makes sense.

Invite him to help you in all you do and he will show you which way to go.'

Scarlet thought about her sunflowers.

She thought about how much she liked them.

She remembered how amazing it was that such a great big flower came from a tiny black and white seed and that leaving them alone in the ground was just what they needed.

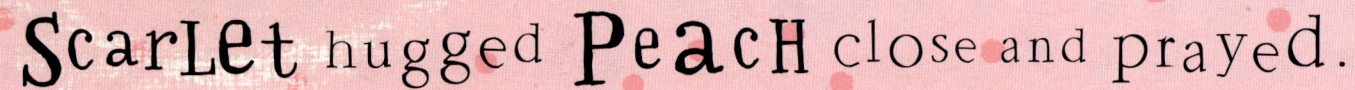

Scarlet hugged Peach close and prayed.

'Thank you God for my sunflowers,
for the seeds and showing me
where to plant them. I would never have
let them grow if it wasn't for you.

Thank you for Peach,
and for my big brown, book.'

'Goodnight Peach,'
said Scarlet.